NORTHWEST
FOREST PLAN
THE FIRST 10 YEARS (1994–2003)

Socioeconomic Monitoring Results
Volume VI: Program Development and Future Directions

Susan Charnley and Claudia Stuart

General Technical Report
PNW-GTR-649 Vol. VI
April 2006

 United States
Department of
Agriculture

 Forest
Service

 Pacific Northwest
Research Station

Authors

Susan Charnley is a research social scientist, U.S. Department of Agriculture, Forest Service, Pacific Northwest Research Station, P.O. Box 3890, Portland, OR 97208. **Claudia Stuart** is a community planner, Mendocino National Forest, U.S. Department of Agriculture, Forest Service, Genetic Resource Center, 2741 Cramer Lane, Chico, CA 95928.

Socioeconomic Monitoring Results
Volume VI: Program Development and Future Directions

Susan Charnley and Claudia Stuart

Northwest Forest Plan—The First 10 Years
(1994–2003): Socioeconomic Monitoring Results

Susan Charnley, Technical Coordinator

U.S. Department of Agriculture, Forest Service
Pacific Northwest Research Station
Portland, Oregon
General Technical Report PNW-GTR-649 Vol. VI
April 2006

Abstract

Charnley, Susan; Stuart, Claudia. 2006. Socioeconomic monitoring results. Vol. VI: Program development and future directions. In: Charnley, S., tech. coord. Northwest Forest Plan—the first 10 years (1994–2003): socioeconomic monitoring results. Gen. Tech. Rep. PNW-GTR-649. Portland, OR: U.S. Department of Agriculture, Forest Service, Pacific Northwest Research Station. 18 p.

The socioeconomic monitoring program of the Pacific Northwest Interagency Regional Monitoring Program went through three phases of development between 1999 and 2005. Volume VI provides a history of the socioeconomic monitoring program, detailing each phase of its development and discussing challenges associated with socioeconomic monitoring at the community scale. Volume VI also evaluates the socioeconomic monitoring plan in the Northwest Forest Plan record of decision, and whether the questions, goals, and monitoring items are still relevant 10 years later. We provide recommendations for future monitoring.

Keywords: Northwest Forest Plan, socioeconomic monitoring, monitoring program history, future monitoring.

Preface

This report is one of a set of reports produced on this 10-year anniversary of the Northwest Forest Plan (the Plan). The collection of reports attempts to answer questions about the effectiveness of the Plan based on new monitoring and research results. The set includes a series of status and trends reports, a synthesis of all regional monitoring and research results, a report on interagency information management, and a summary report.

The status and trends reports focus on establishing baselines of information from 1994, when the Plan was approved, and reporting change over the 10-year period. The status and trends series includes reports on late-successional and old-growth forests, northern spotted owl population and habitat, marbled murrelet population and habitat, watershed condition, government-to-government tribal relationships, socioeconomic conditions, and monitoring of project implementation under Plan standards and guidelines.

The synthesis report addresses questions about the effectiveness of the Plan by using the status and trends results and new research. It focuses on the validity of the Plan assumptions, differences between expectations and what actually happened, the certainty of the findings, and, finally, considerations for the future. The synthesis report is organized in two parts: Part I—introduction, context, synthesis, and summary—and Part II—socio-economic implications, older forests, species conservation, the aquatic conservation strategy, and adaptive management and monitoring.

The report on interagency information management identifies issues and recommends solutions for resolving data and mapping problems encountered during the preparation of the set of monitoring reports. Information management issues inevitably surface during analyses that require data from multiple agencies covering large geographic areas. The goal of that report is to improve the integration and acquisition of interagency data for the next comprehensive report.

The socioeconomic status and trends report is published in six volumes. Volume I of the report contains key findings. Volume II addresses the evaluation question, Are predictable levels of timber and nontimber resources available and being produced? The focus of Volume III is the evaluation question, Are local communities and economies experiencing positive or negative changes that may 6+be associated with federal forest management? Volume IV assesses the Plan goal of promoting agency-citizen collaboration in forest management. Volume V reports on public values regarding federal forest management in the Pacific Northwest. Volume VI (this volume) provides a history of the Northwest Forest Plan socioeconomic monitoring program and a discussion of potential directions for the program.

Summary

The socioeconomic monitoring program of the Pacific Northwest Interagency Regional Monitoring Program has been through three phases of development. Phase 1 lasted from 1999 to 2000, and was designed to review available information and recommend a pilot protocol. Phase II—lasting from 2000 to 2002—tested a pilot monitoring protocol and resulted in a set of recommendations for how to undertake socioeconomic monitoring related to the Northwest Forest Plan (the Plan). Phase III, started late in 2002 and ended in 2005 (also a pilot phase), produced the information contained in this monitoring report (volumes I through V). Volume VI provides a history of the socioeconomic monitoring program, detailing each phase of its development.

The Regional Interagency Executive Committee (RIEC) has not formally incorporated socioeconomic monitoring into the Plan regional monitoring program; nor is there a published socioeconomic monitoring protocol. Following publication of this interpretive report, the RIEC will decide how to proceed with future Plan-related socioeconomic monitoring. To assist with this decision, volume VI evaluates the socioeconomic monitoring plan in the Plan record of decision (ROD) and whether the questions, goals, and monitoring items are still relevant 10 years later. It also provides recommendations for future monitoring.

We find that the Plan goals are still relevant and are consistent with the broader missions and strategic goals of the Forest Service (FS) and the Bureau of Land Management (BLM), although some could be reworded. We also find that the ROD evaluation question that has received most of the program's attention to date—Are local communities and economies experiencing positive or negative changes that may be associated with federal forest management?—should be revised. We recommend formulating monitoring questions that focus on the things that link land management agencies, federal forests, and rural communities and economies in ways that can produce positive outcomes for community well-being and forest ecosystem health.

Contents

Chapter 1: Module History

Introduction

The socioeconomic monitoring program of the Pacific Northwest Interagency Regional Monitoring Program has developed through three phases. The first socioeconomic monitoring team was formed in 1997, but it did not begin monitoring-related work until 1999. Phase I was from 1999 to 2000, phase II from 2000 to 2002, and phase III began in late 2002 and is still underway. The monitoring results in this report (volumes I through V) come from phase III.

Phase I was designed to review available information and recommend a pilot monitoring protocol. Phases II and III were pilots for the monitoring program. The Regional Interagency Executive Committee (the RIEC)[1] has not yet officially incorporated socioeconomic monitoring into the Regional Monitoring Program, nor has a formal protocol been published for socioeconomic monitoring. The monitoring during phase III followed a protocol developed by the socioeconomic monitoring team (the team) in late 2002. The protocol was pilot-tested in 2003–05. If the Committee formally adopts socioeconomic monitoring as part of the Regional Monitoring Program, the team will publish an updated monitoring protocol.

As stated in the Plan record of decision (ROD), "The monitoring plan will be periodically evaluated to ascertain whether the monitoring questions and standards are still relevant, and will be adjusted as appropriate. Some monitoring items may be discontinued and others added as knowledge and issues change with implementation" (USDA and USDI 1994b). Given that two pilot phases have occurred and that the committee must decide the future of Plan-related socioeconomic monitoring, evaluating the socioeconomic monitoring plan in the ROD; judging whether the questions, goals, and monitoring items are still relevant 10 years later; and assessing future options to ensure that agencies have the socioeconomic information they need to support adaptive management in the Plan area are timely.

Chapter 1 begins with an overview of previous efforts at socioeconomic monitoring of forest-based communities, followed by a history of the Plan's socioeconomic monitoring module, documenting its development since 1997. Chapter 2 contains recommendations and options for future socioeconomic monitoring associated with the Plan.

Previous Socioeconomic Monitoring of Forest-Based Communities

One challenge the monitoring team faced in developing a protocol for socioeconomic monitoring was a lack of models. The Northwest Forest Plan's (the Plan) record of decision (ROD) specifically called for monitoring rural economies and communities as part of a regional monitoring strategy. The Forest Service (FS) and the Bureau of Land Management (BLM) had done little in the way of community-scale socioeconomic monitoring in support of forest management before this effort. Although the National Forest Management Act (1976) calls for monitoring forest plans, the focus is typically on implementation monitoring (Wright et al. 2002: 2), and it rarely includes socioeconomic effectiveness monitoring. The FS has been actively involved in socioeconomic monitoring relating to forest sustainability at the national scale as a part of the Montreal Process Working Group on Criteria and Indicators for the Conservation and Sustainable Management of Temperate and Boreal Forests. The FS also regularly assesses trends in the supply of, and demand for, renewable natural resources and recreation at the national and broad regional scales, as mandated by the 1974 Forest and Rangeland Renewable Resources Planning Act. This work does not provide guidance for community-scale monitoring.

A regional FS monitoring effort that included a sociocultural module was initiated in the mid-1990s as part of California's Sierra Nevada framework planning effort. This effort included a conceptual model as a foundation for monitoring an array of environmental, social, economic, and cultural trends across the Sierra Nevada (Manley et al. 2000). The team designed rangewide sampling strategies based on the conceptual framework, including detailed strategies for monitoring change in cultural resources and the implementation and effectiveness of tribal relations programs.

---

[1] The RIEC is responsible for ensuring the prompt, coordinated, and successful implementation of the Northwest Forest Plan at the regional scale and also oversees the Plan's monitoring program and adaptive management processes. The Intergovernmental Advisory Committee advises the RIEC.

Funding and implementing the Sierra Nevada monitoring program concentrated on ecological resources, however.

In 1999, the FS began a pilot study—the Local Unit Criteria and Indicators Development test—to assess how feasible monitoring ecosystem sustainability at the forest scale would be (Wright et al. 2002). The study focused on developing a set of criteria and indicators for monitoring sustainability, including the sustainability of socioeconomic systems, in support of adaptive ecosystem management and forest planning. The result was a monitoring framework containing a core set of criteria and indicators for sustainability monitoring. The pilot national forests in the study conducted community-level socioeconomic monitoring to test the indicators. Some have adopted the final framework and begun implementing monitoring activities in communities around their forests. Other FS monitoring efforts have focused on ecological monitoring (e.g., the Forest Inventory and Analysis Program, Maddox et al. 1999, Mulder et al. 1999, Tolle et al. 1999) rather than socioeconomic monitoring, and they are typically conducted at the broad scale. The BLM has not previously conducted socioeconomic monitoring at the community scale (McElroy 2005).

Outside the FS and BLM, a few models of community-based socioeconomic monitoring relate to forest management.[2] Some researchers have developed frameworks of social and economic indicators that can be used for monitoring sustainability and well-being in natural resource-based communities (such as Beckley and Burkosky 1999, Force and Machlis 1997, Parkins 1999, Parkins et al. 2001). More often than not, these research efforts conclude by identifying a set of socioeconomic indicators to be used in monitoring and stop short of applying them in monitoring programs and of reporting monitoring results useful for adaptive ecosystem management. Consequently, although they provide guidance for what to monitor, they do not provide guidance for how to monitor, nor do they demonstrate how monitoring results can be applied in the resource management context.

Some researchers have developed frameworks of social and economic indicators that have been used in conducting broad-scale assessments in support of forest planning. Several excellent examples demonstrate the use of such indicators in assessing social and economic conditions and trends, community well-being, resiliency, and capacity[3] (Christensen et al. 1999, Doak and Kusel 1996, FEMAT 1993, Harris et al. 2000, Struglia et al. 2001, Sturtevant and Horton 2000). Although such assessments have not been developed within a monitoring framework, they do provide a frame of reference for building an approach to socioeconomic monitoring.

Related research focuses on how to conduct "multi-party" monitoring[4] and "community-based" monitoring[5] in support of ecosystem management (Bliss et al. 2001, USDA 2003). For example, the FS, in collaboration with partner organizations, has developed handbooks for multi-party monitoring of community forest restoration projects (http://www fs fed.us/r3/spf/cfrp/monitoring/). Our monitoring approach does not entail multiparty monitoring, although we consider it to be an option for the future.

The best examples we found of socioeconomic monitoring relating to forests and communities came from the Watershed Research and Training Center in Trinity County, California (Danks et al. 2002) and the Ecosystem Workforce Program at the University of Oregon (Moseley and Wilson 2002). This work was highly influential in developing the monitoring approach used in phase III.

Given the scarcity of existing models to draw from in developing a socioeconomic monitoring program for the Plan area, the history of the Plan's program is one of developing and testing different approaches.

---

[2] Some examples of socioeconomic monitoring are associated with community sustainability projects, conservation and development projects, and certification programs, however.

[3] Community capacity may be defined as the collective ability of community residents to respond to external and internal stress, take advantage of opportunities, adapt and respond to a variety of circumstances, and meet the needs of residents (Kusel 2001: 374).

[4] Multiparty monitoring consists of monitoring by a mixed group of people who are affiliated with local communities, local, regional, or national interest groups, and public agencies (USDA 2003: 3).

[5] Community-based monitoring refers to monitoring activities designed to produce information on social and ecological factors affecting a community that is needed or desired by the community, and in which members of the community participate (Bliss et al. 2001: 145).

Socioeconomic Monitoring Program History

In 1993, President Clinton convened the Forest Ecosystem Management Assessment Team (FEMAT 1993) as part of the effort to develop the Plan. The team was charged with identifying management alternatives for Pacific Northwest federal forests that would maximize social and economic benefits from the forests, while complying with environmental laws and regulations (FEMAT 1993: ii). The FEMAT social assessment found that many communities in the Pacific Northwest were undergoing economic and social transitions from timber dependence to other types of economies. Time limitations imposed on FEMAT precluded a complete investigation of these and other changing dynamics across Pacific Northwest communities.

Given the complex, ongoing changes in the region's forest-based communities, the Forest Service's Pacific Northwest Research Station initiated a program to study rural development in the Pacific Northwest. The program focused on improving knowledge of the region's changing rural places. Researchers sought to better understand contemporary rural social and economic dynamics, to clarify relations between natural resource management and rural communities, and to investigate rural social values (Christensen 2003). Program scientists characterized rural conditions across the Pacific Northwest at the county and larger scales, using data available from the U.S. Bureau of the Census, Bureau of Economic Analysis, state employment departments, and other sources (Christensen et al. 2000; McGinnis et al. 1996, 1997; Raettig 1999, Raettig et al. 1996, 1998). The program also assessed the effectiveness of the Northwest Economic Adjustment Initiative (Christensen et al. 1999, Raettig and Christensen 1999). These efforts, however, did not specifically respond to the socioeconomic monitoring charge contained in the ROD.

Phase I

In 1997, the Regional Ecosystem Office (the REO)[6] initiated an effort to respond directly to the ROD requirement for socioeconomic monitoring. An interagency team was formed to develop a monitoring protocol. The team included social scientists, economists, and others from the Station, the U.S. Army Corps of Engineers, the U.S. BLM, the U.S. FS Pacific Northwest Region (Region 6), and the U.S. Geological Survey's Forest and Rangeland Ecosystem Science Center. The team investigated options for developing the monitoring program.

In 1999, the team commissioned researchers at the University of Washington's Northwest Policy Center and College of Forest Resources to undertake a two-part study. The objectives for the first phase of work were to establish a monitoring framework, undertake preliminary data collection, and estimate the feasibility and costs of completing the evaluation in a succeeding phase of the work. This phase of the project focused solely on the monitoring question in the ROD that pertained to well-being in rural communities and economies, and how that was linked to federal forest management policy. The team also considered the need to develop the monitoring protocol for broader or long-term applications.

The report that resulted from the phase I efforts (Sommers 2001) found that the literature dealing with rural development, socioeconomic assessment, and community effects studies did not offer a proven model for relating forest management to social and economic change. Nor did published data allow researchers to discern the causes of socioeconomic change. County data, such as mill employment, was readily available but could not be used to attribute the causes of change, because it described variables subject to a host of influences. For example, workers commute across county lines from home to workplace, and firms import and export products across county boundaries. Changing technology and business conditions further complicate analysis. These leakages and other confounding

---

[6] The REO supports Plan decisionmaking processes, and implementation of Plan standards and guides.

factors make using existing county data to attribute changes in employment to federal forest management impossible.

A second disadvantage is that county data do not reflect conditions and trends taking place at the community scale, which can differ greatly within a single county. Accordingly, Sommers proposed a conceptual model of local economic flows that related changing forest management to community-scale socioeconomic change. Federal forest management actions were linked directly to local and nonlocal firms, to local workers and their household incomes, and to local services. Federal management was linked indirectly to variables such as income tax revenues and consumption, health, crime, and social capital.

Once estimated by using appropriate data, such a model can establish whether federal actions were the probable cause of socioeconomic changes at the community scale, or whether local change was more likely due to other factors. In addition to validating (or disqualifying) these relations, the data used to estimate the model could also describe change in community socioeconomic characteristics. The approach thus responded to the dual aspects of the ROD socioeconomic monitoring charge: to establish whether local communities and economies are undergoing change, and to discern whether that change is associated with federal forest management.

Sommers also undertook preliminary data collection by using county indicators readily available from secondary sources to describe socioeconomic trends in the Plan area. The available data suggested that the Pacific Northwest's metropolitan economies were stronger than its rural economies during the 1990s.

Sommers identified a complex set of issues associated with estimating and using the local model to determine cause-and-effect relations. Estimating the model would require assembling a substantial amount of community data. Community data, however, were not readily available. Accordingly, Sommers recommended primary data collection by using surveys or interviews to properly estimate the model. To control the increased monitoring costs associated with primary data collection, he suggested a limited sample of community cases.

Which communities should be sampled? More than 1,300 nonmetropolitan communities have been delineated in the Plan area (volume III, chapter 2). Monitoring every community is impractical; yet drawing generalizations about communities regionwide based on a sample is also difficult because the communities are unique. Sommers recommended monitoring a sample of communities typed and paired according to population size, distance from transportation corridors, and type of economic base. Such an approach would allow researchers to generalize results by community type. Alternatively, monitoring could sample a limited set of local communities before and after change in federal forest management. Given this emphasis on local data collection, Sommers also recommended evaluating available county data every 3 to 5 years to monitor regionwide conditions.

Phase II

The second phase of the project was designed to test and evaluate the approaches outlined in phase I. Researchers adopted separate survey instruments for local businesses and households (Sommers et al. 2002). The business survey was to capture information describing economic activity and linkages critical to estimating the local economic model. The household survey was developed to inform the social components of the model and to build a picture of community social capital. When tested, however, the household survey imposed a substantial time burden on test subjects, requiring more than an hour to complete. Researchers estimated the costs of administering the surveys at over $50,000 per community. The need to track potentially large numbers of residents moving into or out of the community during the study period entailed additional costs and challenges. Individual and household privacy were also concerns.

In addition to surveys, the researchers tested a case-study approach using available socioeconomic indicator data together with interviews. They conducted interviews with community members and supplemented them with data published by the U.S. census, local service providers, and others. The economic side of the analysis relied on economic-base theory applied at the subcounty scale.

The test was in Forks, Washington. Peer review indicated that, although community-scale analysis can result in more useful information than county-scale analysis, the monitoring methods tested presented significant limitations. Foremost were the lack of a proven basis for relating local economic change to change in regional federal forest management policy, and relating local economic change to local social change. Reviewers recommended that the monitoring effort focus initially on improving understanding of these relations. They also noted the need for a rigorous method of delineating community boundaries to facilitate community monitoring, given the debate in the literature about how to define a "community" as a unit of analysis.

The phase II report (Jackson et al. 2004) provided the researchers' recommendations for Plan-related socioeconomic effectiveness monitoring. The report noted that a case-study approach incorporating community-scale socioeconomic indicators can be adequate for local socioeconomic monitoring. To validate causal relations between forest management and local communities, however, the report recommended longitudinal business and household surveys by using a sampling strategy based on community cases paired by type and degree of relation to the forest. The monitoring challenges identified by the University of Washington researchers and their key recommendations for how to proceed following phases I and II are summarized here.

Monitoring challenges —
* Determining an appropriate unit of analysis for monitoring (such as county vs. community).
* Defining and delineating "community" as a unit of analysis.
* Selecting sample communities and generalizing from the sample.
* Identifying relevant indicators for which community-scale data are available.
* Investing time and money for primary data collection.
* Distinguishing the effects of forest management policy on communities from the effects of other social, economic, and ecological processes.

Monitoring recommendations from phases I and II —
* Do not limit monitoring efforts to assessing indicators for which data exist from secondary sources.
* Conduct long-term community case studies.
* Define communities operationally according to geographic patterns of employment and retail trade.
* Monitor communities most likely to exhibit impacts from land management activities.
* Survey individuals, households, and businesses over time.

Through the remainder of 2002, the interagency committee responsible for developing the socioeconomic monitoring module considered the results of phases I and II in the context of the literature and evolving methods. Focal considerations were methods both to improve understanding of local community-forest relations, and to describe socioeconomic conditions and trends in rural communities across the Pacific Northwest.

A third phase of the monitoring program began developing in late 2002. The team's charge expanded to include evaluating the second question contained in the ROD: whether predictable amounts of timber and non-timber resources were available and being produced. The team also adopted new methods to address the question of how federal forest management policy was affecting rural economies and communities.

Phase III used the widely accepted approach of interviews as part of rapid social assessment. Interviews were incorporated into a mixed-methods case-studies approach that also gathered secondary data (e.g., Yin 1994). Phase III adopted specific methods used in recent monitoring efforts (Danks et al. 2002, Moseley and Wilson 2002), as well as emerging approaches to delineating communities (Doak and Kusel 1996, Donoghue 2003, Kusel 1996). Monitoring was consistent with recommendations from phases I and II:
* Do not limit monitoring to an assessment of county-scale social and economic indicator data; these data do not reveal community-scale conditions and changes and, although they may be readily available, they are not always relevant for answering the monitoring question.

- Adopt a forest-community case-study approach to relate community-scale social and economic change to changes in federal forest management policy.
- Use a rigorous method of delineating community boundaries to facilitate community-scale monitoring.

- Combine community-scale social and economic indicator data from secondary sources with primary data collection by using surveys or interviews in a sample of communities.

The phase III approach and methods are outlined in detail in volumes II through V of this report.

Chapter 2: Future Direction

The information in this interpretive report is largely the result of retrospective monitoring. No socioeconomic monitoring program was established early in the Northwest Forest Plan (the Plan) period. Thus there was no opportunity to formulate monitoring questions, identify appropriate indicators for answering those questions, and gather monitoring data associated with the indicators over the course of a decade to compile and evaluate in this interpretive report. To a large extent, the monitoring team had to rely on existing data from secondary sources to answer the evaluation questions in the record of decision (ROD) and to evaluate success in meeting Plan socioeconomic goals. These data and their associated indicators were not always adequate for the task. There is now an opportunity to establish a formal socioeconomic monitoring program that identifies relevant monitoring questions with appropriate indicators and to gather monitoring data pertinent to the indicators so that the questions can be answered. This chapter contains our recommendations for future socioeconomic monitoring.

Effectiveness monitoring asks, "To what extent are the goals and objectives of the Plan being achieved?" (Mulder et al. 1999: exec. summary). These goals form the basis for generating questions that the monitoring program should answer (Mulder et al. 1999: 5). We agree: effectiveness monitoring questions should be structured around Plan goals and should evaluate how well those goals are being achieved by identifying trends in associated indicators. However, as Noon et al. (1999: 25) pointed out, information about changes in the status of an indicator by itself is of limited value. Without understanding what is causing monitoring trends, and how management policies versus other variables drive them, we don't know what policies and programs are working, what aren't, and how to effect change in the context of adaptive management. Although monitoring typically results in a description of the status and trends in the attributes being monitored, it also generates information that can be used to build hypotheses about causation that can be tested through research (Busch and Trexler 2003: 4–5). Thus, another thing to consider as the program looks ahead is, how can research be integrated into monitoring to better understand the cause-and-effect relations that underlie monitoring trends?

The agencies' role, not the monitoring team's, is to identify the social and economic goals of federal forest management under the Plan. To help with that process, we review the Plan's socioeconomic goals and their relevance 10 years later and examine the ROD evaluation questions in light of these goals. To provide context, it is worth reviewing the mission and broader management goals and principles of the Forest Service (FS) and Bureau of Land Management (BLM) that are relevant to socioeconomic monitoring.

A part of the FS mission is providing technical and financial assistance to communities to improve their natural environment by caring for their forests; helping communities use forests to promote rural economic development and a quality rural environment; and providing work, training, and education to the unemployed, underemployed, elderly, youth, and disadvantaged in pursuit of the agency mission (http://www.fs.fed.us/aboutus/mission.shtml). Two of the agency's guiding principles are to form partnerships to achieve shared goals and to promote grassroots participation in agency decisions and activities. The 2004 Forest Service Planning Rule calls for understanding the social and economic contributions that FS-managed lands make by evaluating relevant economic and social conditions and trends during the planning process. It also states that national forest lands should contribute to sustaining social and economic systems within their plan areas. The FS 2004 Planning Rule identifies sustainability as the overall goal of land management planning and recognizes that the social, economic, and ecological components of sustainability are interdependent. The rule also calls for a collaborative and participatory approach to planning.

Two of the guiding principles for achieving the BLM mission are to understand the social and economic context in which the agency manages its lands, including the effects of changing social and environmental conditions on land uses and local communities, and to work in partnership with others to achieve a shared vision of how the land and its use will change over time (USDI 2000: 10). One of the BLM's goals is to serve current and future publics, and another is to provide economic and technical assistance to state, tribal, and local governments (USDI 2000: 49). Another BLM goal is to restore and maintain the health of the lands it manages. To understand and plan for the condition and use of BLM lands, the agency recognizes the need for information about the sustainability of land use activities on BLM districts, and their contribution to local and regional socioeconomic conditions (USDI 2000: 54).

Plan Goals: Are They Still Relevant?

The team identified five Plan socioeconomic goals for effectiveness monitoring:

- Produce a predictable and sustainable supply of timber sales, nontimber forest resources, and recreation opportunities.
- Maintain the stability of local and regional economies on a predictable, long-term basis.
- Where timber sales cannot proceed, assist with long-term economic development and diversification to minimize adverse effects associated with job loss.
- Protect forest values and environmental qualities associated with late-successional, old-growth, and aquatic ecosystems.
- Promote interagency collaboration and agency-citizen collaboration in forest management.

Are these goals still relevant and worth monitoring?

Produce a Predictable and Sustainable Supply of Timber Sales, Nontimber Forest Resources, and Recreation Opportunities

Monitoring resource and recreation outputs from federal forest lands is important, because timber sales, nontimber resources, and recreation opportunities provide important social, economic, and cultural benefits to forest-based communities. An important finding of the FEMAT report was that communities wanted stability, predictability, and certainty in timber supplies. Predictability in resource and recreation outputs may be difficult to achieve, however, given the complex and dynamic nature of natural, social, and economic systems—all of which influence the agencies'

abilities to produce a predictable supply of resources and recreation. Agencies may wish to assess what is a realistic goal for the production of timber and nontimber resources that will meet the needs of the public, and reframe this goal accordingly.

Timber sales, nontimber forest resources, and recreation opportunities are not the only socioeconomic benefits that federal forests and their managing agencies provide. They also provide a host of other benefits that the team monitored, such as jobs and income associated with resources and recreation; agency jobs; jobs created through procurement contracting, grants and agreements; community economic assistance funding; and county revenue-sharing programs. A broader view of the socioeconomic benefits that forests provide could be incorporated into this goal statement, for example, "maximize the economic and social benefits from the forests, while conserving forest ecosystems," which was President Clinton's intent with the Plan (USDA and USDI 1994a: volume II E-4). Such a goal is still relevant today. Timber and nontimber resources, recreation, and the other benefits listed here could be specified as monitoring items associated with this goal.

Maintain the Stability of Local and Regional Economies on a Predictable, Long-Term Basis

The purpose of the first goal—to produce a predictable and sustainable supply of timber and nontimber resources—was to help maintain the stability of local and regional economies on a predictable, long-term basis. A finding of this monitoring report is that, although stable timber supplies may contribute to economic stability, they do not ensure it. Assuming that community stability depends on non-declining, even flows of timber from federal forests can be misleading: many factors can influence the stability of forest-based communities. Consequently, the concept of community stability has been replaced by the concept of community resiliency—the ability of communities to respond and adapt to change in positive, constructive ways to mitigate the effects of change on the community (Harris et al. 2000: 6).

Agencies may wish to reframe this Plan goal in light of these findings. A more appropriate goal, linked to the first, might be "provide social and economic benefits that contribute to community well-being, and help communities improve their capacity to adapt to change."

Where Timber Sales Cannot Proceed, Assist With Long-Term Economic Development and Diversification to Minimize Adverse Effects Associated With Job Loss

The Plan sought to mitigate the effects of reduced federal timber sales by assisting with community economic development and diversification through the Northwest Economic Adjustment Initiative. The initiative has ended, and the FS no longer has appropriated funds to support Jobs-in-the-Woods or the Rural Community Assistance Program. Community assistance programs are one means of achieving this goal, but there are also other mechanisms for assisting communities with economic development and diversification. Agency efforts to promote this goal can have positive benefits for forest stewardship.

For example, one Plan objective was to integrate forestry and economic assistance by linking ecosystem management on federal forest lands with local family-wage jobs that would contribute to sustainable communities. Strategies designed to achieve this objective included Jobs-in-the-Woods, land management procurement contracting, and initiative projects that supported recreation and tourism development, and sustainable forestry enterprises, such as small businesses that produce value-added wood products made from small-diameter wood and hardwoods from federal forests. This goal remains as important and relevant today as it was when the Plan was developed.

One of the foremost issues of concern related to forest management expressed by community members interviewed for this study was the lack of family-wage jobs in their communities, especially jobs tied to forest resources. Many community residents interviewed were from families who had a history of working in the woods, and who were struggling to stay and raise their families in the communities they considered home. Residents of forest communities can potentially help forest managers meet their management

objectives given the recent climate of declining agency staff and budgets. Increasing federal forest-based employment opportunities would make an important contribution to community well-being. The desire for forest-based, family-wage jobs was a top priority in the case-study communities monitored, especially those not located near regional centers or urban areas that provide commuting options. The importance of sustaining family-wage, forest-based jobs in rural communities was also acknowledged in regional public surveys (see volume V). Linking forest restoration work with local job creation to promote economic development and diversification in communities is relevant, important, and possible.

Protect Forest Values and Environmental Qualities Associated With Late-Successional, Old-Growth, and Aquatic Ecosystems

Several agency managers have questioned whether the socioeconomic monitoring team should conduct effectiveness monitoring relating to this goal. Some view it as a biophysical goal that should be monitored only by the biophysical modules. We assessed this goal for two reasons.

First, protecting forest values and environmental qualities associated with late-successional, old-growth (older forest), and aquatic ecosystems is a social value. Changes in societal values can trigger the adaptive management process (USDA and USDI 1994a Volume II: E4). Monitoring how public attitudes, beliefs, and values relating to forest management change over time is important, so that managers can be responsive. Second, people's perceptions of the effectiveness of agency management policies can influence their behavior and their attitudes toward the agencies. This information supplements, but does not replace, biophysical monitoring related to this goal.

In our view, the monitoring questions that continue to be relevant are:

* What forest values and environmental qualities associated with federal forests are important to members of the public, and what is the balance of values (both commodity and noncommodity) that members of the public believe federal forests should be managed for?

- How well has federal forest management under the Plan provided for the forest values and environmental qualities that are important to members of the public?

Promote Interagency Collaboration and Agency-Citizen Collaboration in Forest Management

President Clinton wanted federal agencies to work together to achieve Plan goals (USDA and USDI 1994b: 3). The Plan directed federal agencies to coordinate and cooperate in forest management. A host of new institutions and processes were created to improve interagency coordination and communication and to eliminate duplication (Tuchmann 1996: 6–7). The Plan also called for more collaboration between agencies and members of the public in forest management.

The socioeconomic monitoring team did not monitor interagency collaboration under the Plan because we did not have the resources. If interagency collaboration is viewed as an important subject for monitoring, it would be appropriate for the team to do so, and possible if resources were available.

The team did some monitoring of agency-citizen collaboration. We believe it is important and relevant to continue monitoring agency-citizen collaboration in forest stewardship. The FS units appear to rely increasingly on partnerships, volunteers, and joint forest stewardship efforts to get their work done because they lack the budgets and staff to accomplish all of the work themselves. The BLM also emphasizes cooperative partnerships for restoring and maintaining the health of the land. The success of these efforts depends in part on the capacity of communities to engage in them. Interviews with community members showed that many local residents have sophisticated perceptions of complex ecological processes and relations. Interviews also showed that many community members care deeply about nearby forests and their ecological integrity. Although many communities have limited capacity to engage with managers in forest stewardship activities, most communities have some capacity to do so. Agency-citizen collaboration provides one indicator of agency and community capacity and relations. Monitoring also provides insight into what kinds of collaborative arrangements are most successful, and how to better engage in agency-citizen collaboration.

Adaptive management areas were an important Plan component that was not systematically monitored by the team. Future monitoring could examine the role of the areas in meeting Plan and unit-level land management and socioeconomic objectives, relating unit-level outcomes to approaches taken to collaboration. This would provide useful information for future management.

Plan Evaluation Questions: Are They the Right Ones?

The socioeconomic monitoring team addressed two evaluation questions from the ROD:

- Are predictable levels of timber and nontimber resources available and being produced?
- Are local communities and economies experiencing positive or negative changes that may be associated with federal forest management?

We discuss these in turn.

Are Predictable Levels of Timber and Nontimber Resources Available and Being Produced?

The question has two components, one having to do with predictability and one with availability. We did not monitor whether predictable levels of resources and recreation were available because we did not have the capacity to do so; we focused on whether predictable levels of resources were being produced. We believe monitoring resource and recreation outputs from federal forests is important, but the concept of predictability is problematic. Modification of this evaluation question will depend on how that goal is framed. Potential modifications could be: What were the trends in timber sales, special forest products harvested, grazing, mining, and recreation opportunities on federal forest lands? What amounts of timber and nontimber resources are being produced, and how does the Plan (vs. other factors) influence those amounts? Are opportunities to harvest timber, use nontimber resources, and engage in recreation on federal forest lands predictable?

The ROD currently states that timber sales, special forest products, grazing, minerals, recreation, commercial fishing, and scenic quality should be monitored. We recommend dropping commercial fishing as a monitoring item because many factors affect commercial fishing, and we found that evaluating how the Plan might have influenced it was impossible. The Aquatic and Riparian Effectiveness Monitoring Program is evaluating watershed conditions, which are relevant for commercial fishing. Scenic quality is a relevant monitoring item because of its importance for recreation, and because it is one of the amenity values that draw people and businesses to rural communities. The ability to monitor it will depend on data availability (see volume II, app. A).

The agencies might also consider whether other monitoring items should and could be added to the list, such as indicators of ecosystem services and other amenity values.

Although monitoring resource and recreation outputs from federal forest lands is important, doing so is problematic, as volume II of this report demonstrates. Some of the problems the team encountered in evaluating this question were the following:

- Indicators tracked by the agencies were not always the right ones for answering the monitoring question.
- Historical data, in particular, are hard to get, because many of them are not stored in electronic format or in corporate databases.
- The FS regions, and the FS and BLM track some indicators differently, so aggregating agency data for the Plan area as a whole is difficult.
- Existing data are sometimes incomplete, and the numbers provided by regional and state offices, and by local forest units, for the same indicators sometimes differ.
- The direction we were given in evaluating this question was to obtain all of the monitoring data from the FS regional and BLM Oregon state offices, rather than from individual forest units. This direction limited our ability to obtain data because some data are available from local units only.

- The monitoring team consisted of social scientists, not agency program specialists with expertise in the areas of timber, special forest products, recreation, grazing, and minerals. The team had to rely on agency program specialists to help us retrieve, analyze, and interpret the data. Although most of the program specialists invested a great deal of time and effort assisting us, a few were less responsive, making it difficult to obtain data and use the benefit of their expertise. And, there were many instances of reviewers questioning whether our claims about data availability for different indicators were accurate and whether our interpretations of the data were correct.

We recommend that the agencies continue to monitor resource and recreation outputs from federal forest lands as part of the monitoring program. Our recommendations on how to do so are as follows:

- Identify what indicators need to be monitored to answer the evaluation question, and track data relevant to those indicators in a systematic, coordinated way between agencies and regions.
- Collect resource data directly from field units, rather than from regional and state offices.
- Charge agency specialists in the timber, special forest products, grazing, minerals, and recreation programs with the responsibility for monitoring associated with this evaluation question to improve accuracy, efficiency, and accountability.

Are Local Communities and Economies Experiencing Positive or Negative Changes That May Be Associated With Federal Forest Management?

We believe that effectiveness monitoring questions should be structured around Plan goals and should evaluate how well those goals are being achieved. This evaluation question is very broad, general, and not tied to a specific Plan goal that can be evaluated for effectiveness. Moreover, it is difficult to measure the extent to which federal forest management policy, versus other variables, contributes to positive or negative change in communities. Finally, the ROD gives a list of monitoring items associated with this question, several of which we found were impractical or irrelevant to monitor.

We believe the question, "Are communities experiencing positive or negative changes that may be associated with federal forest management" is the wrong one to be asking now. The question stemmed from concern in the early 1990s about how cutbacks in federal timber production would affect forest-based communities. Reduced federal timber harvests have been in place for over 10 years, and are unlikely to change much in the near future. Instead, we believe that monitoring should focus on those forest management policies, programs, projects, and practices—whether initiated by forest management agencies or local communities—that have already been identified through research as potentially making a positive contribution to both community well-being and forest health. Monitoring would focus on the key linkages between forests and communities that have the potential for positive outcomes for the agencies, forest landscapes, and community well-being. Monitoring could help evaluate whether those linkages are becoming stronger or weaker over time; their socioeconomic outcomes for communities; their stewardship outcomes for federal forests; and the causal factors underlying observed trends. Monitoring could also track agency and community capacity to engage in the kinds of mutually-beneficial relations that link healthy forests and healthy communities.

For example, a stable, predictable supply of small-diameter wood is needed to support community investments in technologies and businesses that utilize small-diameter wood, which can lead to reduced community wildfire risk, improvements in ecosystem health, and more jobs and income for communities (COPWRR 2005). Thus, it makes sense to monitor the supply of small-diameter wood coming off of federal forests, community infrastructure development for processing and manufacturing that wood, and jobs and income associated with removing, processing, and manufacturing it. Participatory monitoring of forest resources (such as nontimber forest products)

by community members can contribute to forest managers' knowledge of those resources and help to manage them (Lynch et al. 2004). Participatory monitoring also contributes to harvester knowledge about, and sustainable use of, nontimber forest products. Socioeconomic monitoring could look at community engagement in forest monitoring and its outcomes. A finding of this report is that consistent opportunities to obtain family-wage jobs doing forest restoration work for at least part of the year through agency contracts, grants, or partnership agreements help sustain rural livelihoods. Monitoring agency contracting practices is relevant to understanding contributions to community well-being. Collaboration in joint forest stewardship—such as that which occurs through resource advisory committees, Fire Safe councils, volunteer programs, partnership agreements, and potentially in adaptive management areas—is having some positive outcomes for both communities and forest landscapes; it makes sense to monitor them.

These are just some examples that illustrate the potential for monitoring the variables that link agencies, federal forests, and rural communities and economies in a way that promotes achieving the socioeconomic goals of the Plan: to produce a predictable and sustainable supply of timber, nontimber forest products, and recreation opportunities; to maintain the stability of local and regional economies on a predictable, long-term basis; to assist with long-term economic development and diversification; and, to promote agency-citizen collaboration in forest management. Monitoring these items could also help assess progress toward achieving some of the biophysical goals of the Plan associated with forest protection, ecological restoration, and habitat improvement.

Additional Considerations for Future Monitoring

1. We identified more than 1,300 nonmetropolitan communities in the Plan area. Although communities share commonalities, they are also unique. The Plan affected local communities in different ways because of variation in the conditions associated with Plan implementation on forest units, variation in the

socioeconomic conditions and circumstances in the communities, and variation in the external factors at play in influencing community-scale change. The monitoring results reported here do not do justice to this variation because time and resources only permitted us to sample 4 case forests and 12 communities before preparing this report. Nor was our sample size large enough to permit evaluating some of the expectations contained in the ROD associated with Plan effects. Socioeconomic monitoring should encompass a broader range of forest-community cases in order to adequately capture these differences and to provide a better evaluation of Plan effectiveness for the region as a whole.

We recommend developing a sample of cases to monitor on a rotational basis over a 5- or 10-year monitoring period (depending on program resources). One forest-community case would be selected from each of the 12 planning provinces for long-term monitoring. The number of communities monitored around each case-study forest would differ, depending on how much variation in community "types" and community-forest relations exists.

2. Our assessment of agency effectiveness in meeting Plan goals was based on a regional-scale assessment supplemented by four local-scale examples. We used our results to draw general conclusions in response to the monitoring questions. Generalizations always have exceptions, and undoubtedly, examples could be found that counter our general findings.

Investigating local successes in achieving Plan socioeconomic goals would be useful. Future monitoring should document and profile examples that illustrate how Plan socioeconomic goals are being successfully achieved. These examples could provide useful models and valuable lessons to draw on for adaptive management. For example, in 2005, monitoring around the Okanogan-Wenatchee National Forest identified successes that were unlike those described in this report. A greater depth of monitoring will provide more

complete evaluation of Plan effectiveness and clearer insights into the causes of organizational effectiveness in meeting Plan goals.

Data describing trends in staffing and budgets could also be used to identify units with potentially different institutional capacities. The relations between these units and associated communities could be more closely studied to provide better information on how institutional investments can affect local community outcomes.

3. Socioeconomic monitoring at the local scale would be most efficient and useful if done around forest units undergoing land and resource management plan revision. The case-study monitoring yields social and economic information that supports local planning and management needs, and can provide information for social and economic assessments and impact statements. Northwest Forest Plan-related socioeconomic monitoring could also be coordinated with individual forest plan monitoring. Coordination will improve cost-effectiveness and efficiency and enable local units to maximize their use of monitoring results.

4. To date, the focus of the socioeconomic monitoring program has been on rural communities and economies. This focus excludes metropolitan areas and broader regional stakeholder groups and emphasizes communities of place rather than communities of interest. Forest managers frequently commented that by focusing on rural communities we were missing an important segment of their client population. In evaluating the socioeconomic monitoring program, consideration should be given to whether including metropolitan areas and a wider range of forest stakeholders and communities of interest is important, or whether rural communities and economies should continue to be the focus. This decision will depend on the socioeconomic goals identified.

5. A possible revision of the tribal monitoring protocol is being discussed. Interest has been shown in refocusing that protocol to include questions similar to some

of those investigated by the socioeconomic monitoring team. The socioeconomic and tribal monitoring teams both worked with tribal communities, but not in a coordinated way. Integrating tribal and socioeconomic monitoring is possible because of overlapping interests and areas of inquiry. The agencies may wish to explore how tribal and socioeconomic monitoring could be integrated in the future.

6. The methods that produced the results contained in this monitoring report did not include primary data collection by using surveys. Surveys can provide quantitative monitoring data for a broader geographic area and population than was reached during phase III and may be an appropriate tool for broad-scale socioeconomic monitoring relating to some of the Plan goals. One drawback of surveys is that it can be time-consuming to obtain approval from the Office of Management and Budget to implement them. Nevertheless, the team should consider developing survey methods for future monitoring if the agencies desire socioeconomic data from a larger sample population.

7. The FS has been actively involved in socioeconomic monitoring at the national scale as part of the Montreal Process Working Group on Criteria and Indicators for the Conservation and Sustainable Management of Temperate and Boreal Forests. It would be useful to align some of the socioeconomic monitoring indicators for the Plan area with the Montreal Process social and economic indicators, in order to better link regional- and national-scale socioeconomic monitoring for forest management and sustainability. Not only would this improve national reporting; it would help managers situate regional trends within a national context.

8. The monitoring results reported here were, for the most part, at two scales: the Plan area as a whole, and the community. We sometimes reported results by agency or by state, but for the most part, did not provide an analysis of the spatial distribution of trends at any intermediate scale. Initially the team also intended to report monitoring trends at the province scale (the Plan area is divided into 12 planning provinces). However, this quickly became problematic from a methodological standpoint. The majority of our data are for individual FS and BLM units, or are for counties (an exception being the community-scale U.S. census data). Planning province boundaries do not correspond to national forest or BLM district boundaries; nor do they conform to county boundaries. The methodological complexity of trying to aggregate county and forest-scale data at the province scale given these inconsistencies proved to be more than the team could address for this interpretive report, given time limitations. Nevertheless, we recognize the value of analyzing the spatial distribution of socioeconomic trends and Plan effects across the Plan area, and encourage the team to investigate the potential for analyzing subregional (such as province scale) variation in socioeconomic monitoring trends in the future.

9. Multiparty and community-based monitoring approaches are becoming more widespread for monitoring forest resources and the social and ecological benefits of forest management activities. The advantages of these approaches are that they build trust and relations between stakeholders and management agencies, they raise public awareness and promote public participation in forest management and stewardship, they create an opportunity for participants to contribute their skills and knowledge to improve the monitoring program, they enhance the credibility of the monitoring effort among community members, and they build capacity among participants. Among the drawbacks are that they take time and energy to set up and add organizational complexity to the monitoring process. Nevertheless, if the socioeconomic monitoring program is adopted by the RIEC, the team should consider whether and how multiparty or community-based monitoring methods could be integrated into the program for agency and community benefit.

10. Monitoring produces information that is important for adaptive management, yet it is also a process that can play an important role in building relations between agencies and communities. A common comment the team received from community interviewees was that Plan-related socioeconomic monitoring should have begun much sooner. Just as many community residents felt that forest management under the Plan had failed to produce many of the intended socioeconomic benefits, so they felt that agency monitoring programs that focus on the biophysical components of the Plan have taken precedence over socioeconomic monitoring. This continued emphasis on the biophysical dimension of forest management was perceived as a bias toward the ecological components of the Plan, in contrast to the original Plan intent of balancing ecological and socioeconomic needs. Interviewees welcomed the opportunity to tell their stories and share their perspectives, and wanted them to be heard by the agencies. Investing in socioeconomic monitoring demonstrates that agencies are interested in and care about the social and economic dimensions of forest management, and how federal forest lands can better contribute to community well-being, improving relationships between agencies and communities.

References

Beckley, T.M.; Burkosky, T.M. 1999. Social indicator approaches to assessing and monitoring forest community sustainability. Information Rep. NOR-X-360. Ottawa, ON: Canadian Forest Service, Northern Forestry Centre. 13 p.

Bliss, J.; Aplet, G.; Hartzell, C.; Harwood, P.; Jahnige, P.; Kittredge, D.; Lewandowski, S.; Soscia, M.L. 2001. Community-based ecosystem monitoring. In: Gray, G.J.; Enzer, M.J.; Kusel, J., eds. Understanding community-based forest ecosystem management. Binghamton, NY: Food Products Press: 143–167.

Busch, D.E.; Trexler, J.C. 2003. The importance of monitoring in regional ecosystem initiatives. In: Busch, D.E.; Trexler, J.C., eds. Interdisciplinary approaches for evaluating ecoregional initiatives. Washington, DC: Island Press. 1–23. Chapter 21.

Central Oregon Partnerships for Wildfire Risk Reduction [COPWRR]. 2005. OR Solutions CROP Initiative declaration of cooperation. http://www.coic.org/copwrr/home htm. (April 2005).

Christensen, H. 2003. Personal communication. Research social scientist (retired), Pacific Northwest Research Station, 333 SW First Ave., Portland, OR 97208-3890.

Christensen, H.H.; McGinnis, W.J.; Raettig, T.L.; Donoghue, E.M. 2000. Atlas of human adaptation to environmental change, challenge, and opportunity: northern California, western Oregon, and western Washington. Gen. Tech. Rep. PNW-GTR-478. Portland, OR: U.S. Department of Agriculture, Forest Service, Pacific Northwest Research Station. 66 p.

Christensen, H.H.; Raettig, T.L.; Sommers, P. 1999. Northwest Forest Plan: outcomes and lessons learned from the Northwest Economic Adjustment Initiative. Gen. Tech. Rep. PNW-GTR-484. Portland, OR: U.S. Department of Agriculture, Forest Service, Pacific Northwest Research Station. 98 p.

Danks, C.; Wilson, L.J.; Jungwirth, L. 2002. Community-based socioeconomic assessment and monitoring of activities related to national forest management. Work. Pap. Hayfork, CA: The Watershed Research and Training Center. 36 p. Parts 1 and 2.

Doak, S.C.; Kusel, J. 1996. Well-being in forest-dependent communities: a social assessment focus. In: Sierra Nevada Ecosystem Project: final report to Congress. Davis, CA: University of California, Davis, Centers for Water and Wildland Resources: 375–402. Part 2.

Donoghue, E.M. 2003. Delimiting communities in the Pacific Northwest. Gen. Tech. Rep. PNW-GTR-570. Portland, OR: U.S. Department of Agriculture, Forest Service, Pacific Northwest Research Station. 51 p.

Force, J.E.; Machlis, G.E. 1997. The human ecosystem. Part 2: social indicators in ecosystem management. Society and Natural Resources. 10: 369–382.

Forest Ecosystem Management Assessment Team [FEMAT]. 1993. Forest ecosystem management: an ecological, economic, and social assessment. Portland, OR: U.S. Department of Agriculture; U.S. Department of the Interior [and others]. [Irregular pagination].

Forest and Rangeland Renewable Resources Planning Act of 1974 [RPA]. 16 U.S.C. 1601. (note).

Harris, C.; McLaughlin, W.; Brown, G.; Becker, D.R. 2000. Rural communities in the inland Northwest: an assessment of small rural communities in the interior and upper Columbia River basins. Gen. Tech. Rep. PNW-GTR-477. Portland, OR: U.S. Department of Agriculture, Forest Service, Pacific Northwest Research Station. 120 p.

Jackson, J.E.; Lee, R.G.; Sommers, P. 2004. Monitoring the community impacts of the Northwest Forest Plan: an alternative to social indicators. Society and Natural Resources. 17(3): 223–233.

Kusel, J. 1996. Well-being in forest-dependent communities, part I: a new approach. In: Sierra Nevada Ecosystem Project: final report to Congress, vol. II, assessments and scientific basis for management options. Davis, CA: University of California, Centers for Water and Wildland Resources.

Kusel, J. 2001. Assessing well-being in forest-dependent communities. In: Gray, G.J.; Enzer, M.J.; Kusel, J., eds. Understanding community-based forest ecosystem management. Binghamton, NY: Food Products Press: 359–384.

Lynch, K.A.; Jones, E.T.; McLain, R.J. 2004. Nontimber forest product inventorying and monitoring in the United States: rationale and recommendations for a participatory approach. Portland, OR: Institute for Culture and Ecology. 50 p. http://www.ifcae.org. (March 2005).

Maddox, D.; Poiani, K.; Unnasch, R. 1999. Evaluating management success: using ecological models to ask the right monitoring questions. In: Sexton, W.T.; Malk, A.J.; Szaro, R.C.; Johnson, N.C., eds. Ecological stewardship: a common reference for ecosystem management. Oxford, United Kingdom: Elsevier Science Ltd.: 563–584. Vol. 2.

Manley, P.N.; Zielinski, W.J.; Stuart, C.J.; Keane, J.J.; Lind, A.J.; Brown, C.; Plymale, B.L.; Napper, C.O. 2000. Monitoring ecosystems in the Sierra Nevada: the conceptual model foundation. Environmental Monitoring and Assessment. 64: 139–152.

McElroy, C. 2005. Personal communication. Regional economist, BLM Oregon State Office, 333 SW First Ave., Portland, OR 97205.

McGinnis, W.J.; Phillips, R.H.; Connaughton, K.P. 1996. County portraits of Oregon and northern California. Gen. Tech. Rep. PNW-GTR-377. Portland, OR: U.S. Department of Agriculture, Forest Service, Pacific Northwest Research Station. 315 p.

McGinnis, W.J.; Phillips, R.H.; Raettig, T.L.; Connaughton, K.P. 1997. County portraits of Washington state. Gen. Tech. Rep. PNW-GTR-400. Portland, OR: U.S. Department of Agriculture, Forest Service, Pacific Northwest Research Station. 315 p.

Moseley, C.; Wilson, L.J. 2002. Multiparty monitoring for sustainable natural resource management. Eugene, OR: University of Oregon, Ecosystem Workforce Program. 93 p.

Mulder, B.S.; Noon, B.R.; Spies, T.A.; Raphael, M.G.; Palmer, C.J.; Olsen, A.R.; Reeves, G.H.; Welsh, H.H. 1999. The strategy and design of the effectiveness monitoring program for the Northwest Forest Plan. Gen. Tech. Rep. PNW-GTR-437. Portland, OR: U.S. Department of Agriculture, Forest Service, Pacific Northwest Research Station. 138 p.

National Forest Management Act of 1976 [NFMA]; Act of October 22, 1976; 16 U.S.C. 1600.

Noon, B.R.; Spies, T.A.; Raphael, M.G. 1999. Conceptual basis for evaluating an effectiveness monitoring program. In: Mulder, B.S.; Noon, B.R.; Spies, T.A.; Raphael, M.G.; Palmer, C.J.; Olsen, A.R.; Reeves, G.H.; Welsh, H.H., tech. coords., eds. The strategy and design of the effectiveness monitoring program for the Northwest Forest Plan. Portland, OR.: U.S. Department of Agriculture, Forest Service, Pacific Northwest Research Station: 21–48. Chapter 22.

Parkins, J.R. 1999. Enhancing social indicators research in a forest-dependent community. The Forestry Chronicle. 75(5): 771–780.

Parkins, J.R.; Stedman, R.C.; Varghese, J. 2001. Moving toward local-level indicators of sustainability in forest-based communities. Social Indicators Research. 56: 43–72.

Raettig, T.L. 1999. Trends in key economic and social indicators for Pacific Northwest states and counties. Gen. Tech. Rep. PNW-GTR-474. Portland, OR: U.S. Department of Agriculture, Forest Service, Pacific Northwest Research Station. 30 p.

Raettig, T.L.; Christensen, H.H. 1999. Timber harvesting, processing, and employment in the NWEAI region: changes and economic assistance. Gen. Tech. Rep. PNW-GTR-465. Portland, OR: U.S. Department of Agriculture, Forest Service, Pacific Northwest Research Station. 16 p.

Raettig, T.L.; Christensen, H.H.; Donoghue, E. 1998. The Northwest Economic Adjustment Initiative: an assessment. 148 p. Unpublished report. On file with: Regional Community Economic Revitalization Team, Forest Service, Pacific Northwest Region, P.O. Box 3890, Portland, OR 97208.

Raettig, T.L.; Donoghue, E.; Christensen, H.H.; McGinnis, W.J. 1996. USDA rural development in Oregon: an analysis. Research project report for Rural Development, Oregon State. 141 p. On file with: USDA Rural Development, 101 SW Main, Suite 1410, Portland, OR 97204-3222.

Sommers, P. 2001. Monitoring socioeconomic trends in the northern spotted owl region: framework, trends update, and community level monitoring recommendations. Seattle, WA: U.S. Geological Survey, Forest and Rangeland Ecosystem Science Center, Cascadia Field Station, College of Forest Resources, University of Washington. 56 p. http://www.reo.gov/monitoring/socio/ph1final-body.pdf. (June 2004).

Sommers, P.; Lee, R.G.; Jackson, E. 2002. Monitoring economic and social change in the northern spotted owl region: Phase II—Developing and testing an indicators approach. Draft technical report. 40 p. On file with: U.S. Geological Survey, Forest and Rangeland Ecosystem Science Center, Cascadia Field Station, College of Forest Resources, Box 352100, Seattle, WA 98195-2800.

Struglia, R.; Winter, P.L.; Meyer, A. 2001. Southern California socioeconomic assessment: sociodemographic conditions, projections, and quality of life indices. Riverside, CA: U.S. Department of Agriculture, Forest Service, Pacific Southwest Research Station, Wildland Recreation and Urban Cultures.

Sturtevant, V.; Horton, R. 2000. Revisiting community capacity: five years after FEMAT: insights from case studies of Rogue River National Forest communities. Ashland, OR: Southern Oregon University, Department of Sociology.

Tolle, T.; Powell, D.S.; Breckenridge, R.; Cone, L.; Keller, R.; Kershner, J.; Smith, K.S.; White, G.J.; Williams, G.L. 1999. Managing the monitoring and evaluation process. In: Sexton, W.T.; Malk, A.J.; Szaro, R.C.; Johnson, N.C., eds. Ecological stewardship: a common reference for ecosystem management. Oxford, United Kingdom: Elsevier Science Ltd.: 585–602. Vol. 2.

Tuchmann, E.T.; Connaughton, K.P.; Freedman, L.E.; Moriwaki, C.B. 1996. The Northwest Forest Plan: a report to the President and Congress. Washington, DC: U.S. Department of Agriculture, Office of Forestry and Economic Assistance. 253 p.

U.S. Department of Agriculture, Forest Service [USDA]. 2003. Multiparty monitoring and assessment guidelines for community based forest restoration in southwestern ponderosa pine forests. Albuquerque, NM: Southwestern Region. 91 p. http://www fs fed.us/r3/spf/cfrp/monitoring/. (July 12, 2005).

U.S. Department of Agriculture, Forest Service; U.S. Department of the Interior, Bureau of Land Management [USDA and USDI]. 1994a. Final supplemental environmental impact statement on management of habitat for late-successional and old-growth forest related species within the range of the northern spotted owl. Vol. 1. [Irregular pagination].

U.S. Department of Agriculture, Forest Service; U.S. Department of the Interior, Bureau of Land Management [USDA and USDI]. 1994b. Record of decision for amendments to Forest Service and Bureau of Land Management planning documents within the range of the northern spotted owl. [Place of publication unknown]. 74 p. [plus attachment A: standards and guidelines].

U.S. Department of the Interior [USDI]. 2000. Bureau of Land Management strategic plan. http://www.blm.gov/nhp/info/stratplan/strat0105. [Date accessed unknown].

Wright, P.A.; Colby, J.L.; Alward, G.; Hoekstra, T.; Tegler, B.; Turner, M. 2002. Monitoring for forest management unit scale sustainability: the local unit criteria and indicators development (LUCID) test management edition. IMI Report No. 5. Fort Collins, CO: U.S. Department of Agriculture, Forest Service, Inventory and Monitoring Institute. 41 p.

Yin, R.K. 1994. Case study research: design and methods. Thousand Oaks, California, London, and New Delhi: Sage Publications.